"In his new book Looking and Seeing; Keith Hudson will help you see beyond the natural to truly seeing with your heart. Get your copy today to begin a deeper experience with the Lord and the supernatural."

----JENTEZEN FRANKLIN
SENIOR PASTOR, FREE CHAPEL
AUTHOR OF NY TIMES BEST SELLER, FASTING

"I love this book! Looking and Seeing is such a now word for this generation and those who long to see what God is up to! Keith Hudson has hit the nail on the head; every chapter is loaded with revelation that will stir you up to look past the natural realm so you can see things the way God sees them. Get ready for your life to be radically transformed as you see yourself, others and God's purposes from a whole new perspective!"

-----BETH JONES
PASTOR, VALLEY FAMILY CHURCH
AUTHOR, GETTING A GRIP ON THE BASICS SERIES

"When you first meet Keith Hudson, you will quickly see that there is nothing ordinary about him. From the way he talks, walks, thinks, and yes even dresses. His outward demeanor is a reflection of his inward thinking. Keith Hudson has swag and he thinks big. Whether your challenge is your dream, finances or even your family, Keith believes there is more to life than what you currently see. This book will give you the inspiration and the tools to get up, get going and live beyond what you have seen in the past."

-----TIM STOREY
AUTHOR, COMEBACK & BEYOND:
HOW TO TURN YOUR SETBACK INTO YOUR COMEBACK

"Thank you Keith Hudson for showing us how to open our "heart eyes" so we can move beyond looking to seeing. Looking brings information, but seeing brings transformation. Get ready for real change!"

-----JIM REEVE
SENIOR PASTOR, FAITH COMMUNITY CHURCH

LOOKING &
SEEING

4

ANGELA, SVEND, KATY, DAVID, JENNIFER, BEAU, AND KAI:
TO THE NEXT GENERATION OF SEERS.

LOOKING & SEEING

by Keith Hudson

Arise Publications
of Keith and Mary Hudson Ministries
P.O. Box 50937
Irvine, CA 92619
keithhudson.org
Made in the U.S.A.

Book illistrator Markus "Jake" Filkey

First Edition, 2013

ISBN: 978-1-4675-8447-0

Contents

Acknowledgments | 11

Introduction | 13

1 A MOMENT of TRUTH | 17

2 LOVE and GRATITUDE | 23

3 Seeing BEYOND the NATURAL | 29

4 Seeing YOUR LIFE As it REALLY IS | 35

5 TURN on the LIGHTS | 39

6 Be READY for Your Day of DESTINY | 45

7 CLARITY | 51

8 WALKING by FAITH | 55

9 NOW is the TIME | 63

10 SEERS in the BIBLE | 69

CONCLUSION 73

Acknowledgements

I WANT TO EXTEND A SPECIAL THANK YOU TO MY wonderful wife, Mary. I always say, she is the brains of this ministry but I am the guts.

Thank you to those who have labored to make this book possible, Judi Chimits for her excellence in editing and Jake Filkey for his determined formatting and finishing abilities, as well as our whole KHM ministry team.

And our deep appreciation to our partners who are helping us take the message of Looking and Seeing on the Urgency Tour around the globe.

Introduction

S uddenly, their eyes were opened and they recognized Him." (Luke 24:31 NLT) When tightrope walker Nik Wallenda navigated a section of two inch steel cable across a section of the Grand Canyon in June 2013, he kept his eyes on the prize: the finish line. A camera mounted on his head recorded the 22-minute walk 1,500 feet above the Navajo Indian nation. Wallenda's key to staying steady on his path was to keep his eyes on the goal - and not at the unsteady cable. At times, the cable swayed wildly in the up to thirty mph wind gusts. These unexpected bursts of air drove Wallenda to his knees more than once, but still he did not yield to the raw circumstances. Reminiscent of Peter walking on the water, who kept his eyes on Jesus and was not bothered by the "winds and waves boisterous,

Wallenda remained steady by praying to the Lord over his microphone, lifting up the name of Jesus for the entire world to hear. The Discovery Channel documented the two-hour feat live on prime time without any editing, and it was the highest rated show CNN has had in more than two years. Wallenda's cries of "Thank you Lord, Praise you God," and "Praise You Jesus" did not fall upon deaf ears. At the end of the successful event, CNN's Piers Morgan acknowledged it was a testimony to the power of prayer. Wallenda's determined gaze generated 1.3 million Tweets and 2.1 live streams of the event.

Like this disciplined athlete, you need to learn how to look beyond your present situation and keep your eye on His Presence. God is ready to display His glory in your life as well in these last days, but it is going to take boldness for you to take the mask off and look at people and situations the way God sees them, not how man looks at them. What may stand in front of you may look too big for you to grasp; that what you see now is the way it's always going to be. Or you look at the dream God has given you and think, "there is no way I can ever accomplish this with my resources at my age…" That is the moment you have to flip the switch from looking to seeing.

Walt Disney could have looked at the ferris wheel in Los Angeles' Griffith Park where he took his daughter to play, but instead he started to envision a family playground where parents and children could play together. Out of a little ferris wheel came a 256 billion dollar empire, starting with Disneyland.

The purpose of this book is to draw the "seer" out of you; to coax you into taking a second glance. To start moving on the high wire of your life with greater clarity, to being like that deer with hind's feet that Habakkuk 3:19 describes. That animal's feet look spindly and feeble but they are actually Maserati wheels of maneuverability on the high wire of life.

Why is it so important that you be a seer? Because God is showing He wants you to catch the lighter shades of gray in people and situations that come before you. What lies behind the angry demeanor on that person's face? What is really going on in that teenager's heart? How does God look at that homeless man on the street? Are you making a judgment call based upon a cursory glance at a crusty, tattooed body or pierced body or do you see the potential of passion and mercy as this person works with orphans in garbage dumps in your city, after once his heart is transformed into a new creature in Christ?

The Lord wants to "open the eyes of your understanding to show you what is the hope of your calling…" (Ephesians 1:19 NKJV) You were not put on this earth to pass time but to fulfill His plan. However, you have to recognize see what that plan is in order to accomplish it. This is a day of revelation, not information. We glance quickly at people and sum them up with a "drive-by" decision instead of really seeing what God wants to accomplish in their lives.

One young man was on his way to prison for six months after giving his life to the Lord. Although Christ had been formed in him in between the time the crime was committed and his actual jail sentence, the court had already sentenced him. But the church elders saw a whole new opportunity: send him into an environment they would never be able to penetrate with the gospel themselves. When the man finished his time, over sixty people had given their heart to the Lord. That church didn't look at this young convert as a person with a past, they saw him as a potential evangelist with a future; they prayed over him and sent him into that environment with faith. They saw this opportunity for what it was, an unusual opportunity to win souls in an impenetrable prison. The light always dispels the darkness, when you allow it to; Man looks on the outward appearance but God looks on the heart. He wants you to move into the unseen realm.

You can have all the information in the world. You might be a Nobel Peace Prize winner, a Harvard professor or an MD Anderson cancer researcher, with cutting edge discoveries at your fingertips. But just having knowledge is not enough to be able to see, perceive and understand the mystery of God – understanding what He is really saying to you. You must also have the wisdom to know how to use that knowledge.

Millions live their lives just looking at the idea of a God, but never really understand that God, Jesus and all the angels are real entities who want to spend eternity with us – His people. The Lord wants to be real to you. Do you remember the moment when Christianity became more than an idea to you – when it became a relationship?

Suddenly, you went from looking at life to seeing the Giver of life. You are transformed and you now have a responsibility to see others shift from merely looking at life, to seeing The One who is life. You can help others be transported from natural experience, to what can only be known in the supernatural. As you move from knowledge to wisdom, you are able to do the same for others. And, in doing so, you help others' eyes be opened so they can 'see' for the very first time.

In this book, I want to help you move further into this supernatural realm. My goal with this book is to help you understand the difference between looking and seeing, and change your thinking about the way you see others.

Chapter 1

A MOMENT OF TRUTH

A*fter this I looked, and behold, a door standing open in heaven! And the first voice which I had heard addressing me like [the calling of] a war trumpet said, 'Come up here, and I will show you what must take place in the future." (Revelation 4:1, AMP)* When I read this scripture, the word "looked" stood out to me. At that moment, I experienced a revelation that I want to share with you in this book. The Lord said to me that He wants to take this generation from "looking" to "seeing". So what is the difference, you ask? A pastor can look at his small congregation and get discouraged with discouragement because his numbers are down – but he's looking not seeing. This remnant could be a group of mentoring leaders who will, literally, turn the world upside down, and do what the pastor would never have the time or energy for. Or someone could be looking at their family, health or checkbook wondering how they are going to feed their family of five. Or they could be looking at their child in a coma in intensive care, wondering if she will ever wake up. But God wants them to see that He is more than enough in any situation, and provision and healing are available to them.

There's a real world out there looking for real people in a real church.

Before I was saved, I was a "yippie". A yippie was a radical hippie, who participated in the sixties "peace" marches, when the only peace we had was between our two fingers. My standard attire was a tie-dye t-shirt and patch pants. I always carried 500 tabs of LSD in my back pocket and had three in my system at all times.

One day I was on my way to find work, picking apples on a farm in Wenatchee, Washington. There was a line of us on the freeway ramp, looking to hitchhike a ride. You could wait for days waiting for a lift. And along came this little old gray haired lady in her Volkswagen beetle, and stopped by the side of the road. She waved to me, saying, "Jump in Sonny, I will take you a ways up the road." So I got into the car and she started driving. She didn't say much or even ask my name. But after a few minutes she put one hand on my leg, and the other on the steering wheel, and started to talk in a language I had never heard before.

My mind couldn't fathom what she was doing, and I could have jumped out of the car, thinking she was crazy. I had been on a lot of acid trips before but this was something I had never experienced. In spite of all that, I could see something deeper in her – I knew that she was connecting with God in a way I had never experienced before. Later I realized that she was praying in tongues. When you pray in your heavenly prayer language, it is your spirit praying directly to God the Father. The enemy cannot understand what you say. When she prayed for me, she was praying out mysteries in the spirit, unrolling the plan of my life to meet Him the Father in a very unusual way.

About ten minutes into this unusual encounter, all of a sudden I began to feel a love flood that car that I had been desperate for all my life. The presence of God began to invade that space. I began to weep. I didn't ask her what the presence was, but now I know that little VW bug was overtaken by God's love.

Finally she stopped, leaned over to me and said, "This is as far as I can take you." She reached into the back seat and grabbed a black Gideon Bible and said, "Here, Sonny, read this, it will change your life." Not knowing how to respond to all this, I stumbled out of the car and said "Thank you so much, I appreciate that."

The next day, I started picking apples on the farm. Lugging sixty-pound bags of apples down a ladder hour after hour turned out to be really hard work for a drug-hardened hippie. After a few days of this, I was wiped out. Stumbling down to my cabin, I shook out my backpack onto my bunk, looking for something to read. And there in the pile was that Bible.

I had good parents growing up in Memphis, TN, but all I knew about Christianity was "Jesus loves me, this I know, because the Bible tells me so." Even that little lyric rolling around my head was enough to make me curious enough to pick this book up and start reading it. Everything in those days was psychedelic, so when I opened it up to the New Testament and saw red letters, I thought, 'Wow, Jesus was tripping.'

Three days later, I was still at it. I couldn't put it down. This ancient book was alive and telling me all about my life, where I came from, where I was then, and where I was going. The Holy Spirit had me locked in on His word. I was transfixed. And I wasn't even a good reader. When I graduated from high school a few years before, all the teachers threw their hats off, since they knew that was the last time they would have to put up with me.

Later, on the third day, enough was enough. I was saturated with the Word. Climbing up to the top of a hill I took the Bible and cried out, "God, if you are real, show me!" The pages fell open to Romans 10: 9 & 10. "If you will believe in your heart and confess with your mouth the Lord Jesus, you shall be saved." It was like these words jumped right out of those pages and stood in front of my eyes. Those words broke me through. My spirit became alive in God. Suddenly, I could sense His presence better than any psychedelic drug I had ever taken. The same love that I had experienced in that little Volkswagon enveloped me. I stood there and wept and wept. The more the tears streamed down my face, the more I was being cleansed by the love of God. I knew something had taken place at that very moment.

Walking back down to my cabin, I headed for my bunk. My roommate came into the room, saw my eyes red with tears, and said, "What's wrong, man? Have you been on a bad trip? Are you all right? There is some bad acid out there." I said, "Yes, I am fine," but he kept pressing me, saying "What is going on with you, you look all messed up!" So I told him," Nothing is wrong with me, Jesus Christ has just come into my life."

We need to be grateful and stand up for the Master. You will never grasp so great a salvation until you step over into glory, but you can have an attitude of gratitude and walk boldly as a Christian.

The Bible gave me a whole a new perspective – a new 'take' on life. I began to see things in a light that had never been visible to me before.

Revelation started to be downloaded to me that I had not known or even wanted to understand before. I was no longer looking at my life through dark sunglasses. I was seeing a new path clearly for the very first time.

God has a new dimension for us to walk and to live in. We simply need to ask. Mysteries are unveiled to us as we seek God to show us His ways. Ask God to give you His eyes so that you will see people the way He sees them.

Keith Speak: "You say, 'Brother Hudson, I would never act the way you act.' I say, 'That's your problem–you need to get delivered…from yourself!'"

Imagine bringing a 1975 model television into your home and setting it up. Your children wouldn't know what to do with the rabbit ear antenna on the back and they certainly would wonder what happened to the remote control! Where's the HD? What about TiVo? Where are the 3D glasses? Imagine the surprise on their faces when you tell them they have to get up and change the channel or adjust the volume. Well…that's what is happening in the spirit right now.We are on a fast track spiritually, and the way we did things in 1975, last year, or even last month won't work. We're in the era of 3-D where everything looks more real and it's not only about watching – it's about experiencing!

Just like technology is changing, so is the way we see others. When you see people for who they really are, and you do not just judge them, by the way they look, you are beginning to see life from a whole new vantage point – a brand new perspective. Judging a drug-addicted teen, a husband who is in prison, or a daughter living with her boyfriend is looking at others with a very one-dimensional mindset: that is not how He sees these people. In God's eyes, they are His creation. They are a tangible reminder of the price He paid when He gave His son to die on the cross for you and me. While others may wander off of the path God has set for them, that doesn't mean He loves them any less – and neither should we. God sees their hearts, and knows what it will take to bring them back to Him. Seeing it from His point of view will help you cooperate with His plans.

God looks upon the heart. He not only looks at the heart, but He looks at the heart of the matter. He sees what is going on inside of that person. And, it's easy with our limited vision to look at the surface – you probably do it every day. But when you base your opinions on an external assessment, you aren't seeing the whole picture.

It is like judging a book by the cover, when God says that's not how He sees people. God wants you to turn the pages and see the real condition of someone's spirit.

He is trying to get you to move you into the unseen realm. It is so easy to just look at the surface of a situation in life and not go deeper. But we do not live in a two-dimensional world. We live in three dimensions: body, soul and spirit. We cannot see God in the natural realm, but we can experience His Presence in the supernatural. We hear God through His Word and by hearing Him through those He has called us to serve.

If you've never received Jesus as your Lord and Savior, I want to give you the same opportunity I had years ago. This is a moment where you can ask Him into your heart to be your personal Lord and Savior. Receiving Jesus is not complicated. You don't have to be in church. You simply need to open your heart to Him.

BECOMING A SEER

If you would like to receive Jesus right now, pray this prayer: "Jesus, I admit that I have missed the mark in life. I have sinned and I need your forgiveness. I believe that you are the Son of God. I believe that I am forgiven now, because you shed your blood for me. You took my sin, so I can be right with God. I receive your forgiveness. I receive your love. I receive you into my heart, and invite you to be the Lord of my life. Amen."

Chapter 2

LOVE AND GRATITUDE

Do not look at his appearance or at his physical stature, because I have refused him. For the Lord does not see as man sees; for man looks at the outward appearance, but the Lord looks at the heart." (I Samuel 16:7 NKJV) A few years ago, Mary and I were in Paris. The streets there are very crowded with people bustling and going about their business. In the morning there are literally thousands of people going to work. There are also people begging on the streets. It's common to see the elderly or young mothers with children asking for money. But this day, as we walked along, I saw a young teen sitting with a plastic cup in his hand against the wall.

When I saw him, the Lord spoke to me and said, "You need to see him the way I see him." On the surface, he was a teenager with dirty hair and clothing. Beyond the surface, I saw someone completely beaten-down by life and overwhelmed at his predicament. In that moment, I realized that this young man was someone's son, someone's brother, and very easily, he could've been my child. A lot of people were walking by and around him just looking – but God had something special in mind for me that day – God wanted me to see this young man.

In the hippie movement, I was rejected. I was a long-haired, snaggle toothed young man wearing wild clothes. I was searching for something (I didn't know at the time that I was looking for God). The world rejected me because of the way I looked. However, the Jesus Movement invaded where I was living and literally thousands of hippies gave their lives to the Lord. I was one of them! I knew what it felt like to be rejected and I knew how it felt to be invisible. I couldn't do it to this young man.

I decided to be a radical Christian in that moment! I walked into the nearest café and I grabbed a new plastic cup. I then opened my wallet and filled the cup with all of the Euros I had in my wallet… not just coins bills. I walked out to the young man and I grabbed his worn out cup… then I gave him the new cup filled with all I had. At first he was confused – then he looked inside the cup. I can't begin to express the change on his face in that moment. I didn't give him the Four Spiritual Laws but love flowed out of me. When he looked up at me, I remembered how I felt at the age of 24 when I felt that love for the first time. It flowed from me to him at that moment. He began to weep because someone genuinely cared about him. The anointing began to reach out.

I was reminded of the verse, "Assuredly, I say to you, inasmuch as you did it to one of the least of these My brethren, you did it to Me." (Matthew 25:40). There were people walking by saying, "Look at that young man begging, look at him". But I knew that God wanted me to actually see him.

I said, "When no one cares for you, Jesus does." I know he will never forget that day for the rest of his life. As I walked away, the young man was still weeping under that anointing.

People come from all different backgrounds with all kinds of sins they are caught in. One is not worse than the other. Sin is just missing the mark of His best for your life, but you can get way off base if you do not repent.

This world is not looking at how spiritual you are, but they do want to know, 'Do you love me?' Will you love them even in their imperfection, or will you judge them? The reason you got saved is because someone showed up in your life with of the love of God.

It is God's goodness that led us to repentance. And in reality, what keeps you going is God's love. And His radical love and unconditional forgiveness was the only thing that could get me off drugs and keep me off them.

Have you ever seen two people in love? You can tell they are crazy about each other because the girl scoots all the way over in the truck next to the guy. They look like one body with two heads when you are driving behind their car. You are looking at what looks like one person. But if you get up close and personal, you will see there are actually two heads - two separate people.

If it were not for the love of God, you would not be with Him today. No one strong-armed you into getting saved, or it would not have been from your heart. It was the gentle wooing, a coaxing of the Holy Spirit that drew you to Him. And, if you think about your past, you are probably so grateful that He found you when He did.

Colossians 1:13 in the Jordan translation says, "It was the Father who sprang us from the dominion of darkness, and turned us loose into the new world of His beloved Son."

Has anyone ever had to post bail for you or someone you know, either now or BC (before Christ)? If so, what they were doing was springing you out of jail. That is exactly what Jesus did when He gave Himself for you on the cross! This is what you experienced when you asked Him into your heart. He set you free once and forever.

You were set free from darkness when you walked into His marvelous light and asked Jesus in to your heart. And that is what wisdom and revelation are all about. You don't need more knowledge. You need revelation of the knowledge you already have. This is what seeing truly is: revealed knowledge.

The enemy may have tried everything he could to take you out before your time. You might have been shot, had an overdose of drugs, or been in a car accident. So many situations could have finished you off before you even got started on your born again trail. But, they didn't because God has a plan for you.

It is awesome to think that we will spend all of eternity in heaven with Him because of a simple change of heart. This is so great a salvation. We need to be thankful and grateful God pursued us.

When was the last time you thanked God for working in your life? You may not have experienced the breakthrough you have been praying for yet, but you have to admit you have come a long way since the day you asked Jesus into your heart. That alone is enough to cultivate an attitude of gratitude for what Jesus did for you on the cross!

Have you ever read the story of the ten lepers in Luke 17:11-15? It's worth taking a minute to read through now:

> "As He went on His way to Jerusalem, it occurred that [Jesus] was passing [along the border] between Samaria and Galilee. And as He was going into one village, He was met by ten lepers, who stood at a distance. And they raised up their voices and called, Jesus, Master, take pity and have mercy on us! And when He saw them, He said to them, Go [at once] and show yourselves to the priests. And as they went, they were cured and made clean. Then one of them, upon seeing that he was cured, turned back, recognizing and thanking and praising God with a loud voice..." (AMP)

There were ten lepers who came to Him for healing, but only one came back to thank Jesus for what He had done. These men were deformed from this disease. Their lives had been stolen from them. But only one of them had the ends of his ears, fingers and toes restored, and that was the one who came back to thank Him. And he wasn't quiet about it.

The other lepers were cured of leprosy but still had body parts missing. But because of the tenth one's attitude of gratitude, his diseased extremities were totally restored. He saw that he was healed, but he didn't stop there, he went beyond that and gave thanks.

He saw what the Lord could do for him. His heart was not self-absorbed or having its own pity parties any longer. Instead, he had a servant's heart. He was grateful for what his Master had done for him, and returned to give Jesus glory and honor.

A pastor friend of ours was given a three million dollar gift to pay off his church building by a well-known foundation. The philanthropy that endows such funds to churches and Christian organizations has donated over 53 of these multi-million dollar gifts over the years! However, only three of these non-profits that received these incredibly generous grants ever went back to say 'Thank You' to the President of the group.

They recognized how all their needs had been met in a time of crisis. But they did not look beyond their immediate provision, to be thankful for the incredible kindness of their benefactors.

However, our friend, one of the three recipients that did go beyond the call of duty, actually flew back to the corporation's offices and thanked the CEO personally. This act of appreciation led the corporation's head to tell the grateful recipient he would automatically be approved for a second gift of millions of dollars should he ever need it.

In other words, the next time they decided to upgrade their building and buy a bigger facility, the money was there to pay for it - in full. All because this pastor had remembered to say thank you. He went beyond looking at a surface relationship and did something tangible with his appreciation. Obviously, thankfulness is a precursor to your extended blessing.

There is always someone behind the pen or computer that can push your miracle through for you. The Holy Spirit was the agent that brought that pastor or person across your path to explain to you the way to your breakthrough. Why you, when you don't deserve it? Why are you so favored? God favors those who follow Him with greater revelation.

BECOMING A SEER

As you seek to receive from God, I encourage you to wrap every request in love and gratitude. Cultivate this wonderful attitude of love and thankfulness. As you do, revelation will flood every area of your life!

Thomas Jefferson said, "A man who writes is an exact man." Part of cultivating an attitude of thankfulness is to make note of the things God has done for you. I encourage you to take a few minutes and write down five things areas where God has intervened on your behalf. Be concrete in your thankfulness.

1._____

2._____

3._____

4._____

5._____

Chapter 3

SEEING BEYOND THE NATURAL

S ince we consider and look not to the things that are seen but to the things that are unseen; for the things that are visible are temporal *(brief and fleeting), but the things that are invisible are deathless and everlasting." (II Corinthians 4:18 AMP)* I'm sure you can recall a time when someone has pointed a finger at you and told you what you needed to do. We cannot go to this generation with a finger... we have to go with an open hand. This generation wants to know that we love them and we don't simply judge them – we love and see them the way God sees them: future disciples!

I went to one of my daughter's concerts. You say, "Would you go to a worldly concert?" My answer is absolutely, "YES!" Where do you think Jesus would go? At the venue, I was behind the scenes looking out at the audience of 20,000 screaming fans. They pressed against the fence trying to get closer to the stage because they wanted to get closer to her. All of a sudden I began to weep. This overflowing stadium looked so much like the inside of a church – people with hands raised worshipping – but worshipping the wrong thing. This is a generation that longs to worship. They long to follow and want to be loved but fear of being judged has kept them out of church.

Many churches view judgment as a way to exclude people based upon external factors. That's not God. God loves this generation, and He longs to have them restored to Him. We make choices that separate us from God; we can also make choices that draw us closer to Him.

Jesus isn't about religion – He's about relationship. There are millions in eternity right now who would love to have the opportunity you have to press closer to God. This is a season where you are being called to draw closer to Him. It is easy to get caught up in the day-to-day and forget that there's much more to life than where you are now.

Real faith, 'seeing' faith is an anchor. An anchor on a battleship can weigh up to 40,000 pounds. It has ridged edges that sink into the bottom of the ocean. It can secure a boat carrying five thousand sailors tight until it is time to cast off again and get going. Your faith is like the anchor – it's there to secure you when you need it and it can be lifted when it is time to cast off.

When you start to see something through the eyes of God, it is a real "aha" moment. When you enter the realm of faith you enter a place where anything can happen.

We need revelation in our lives. Revelation about our family, ministry and work. You are not a prisoner of your past. You are not bound by negative words spoken by your relatives and friends. You are not a black sheep who was stuck with affliction, poverty, disease, and lack of promotion, bad marriage, or wayward kids.

You may have been surrounded by people who looked at you on the surface and didn't see you the way God sees you. God sees you as whole person, prosperous, strong, in a loving marriage with anointed and successful children.

Once you redefine the picture with a new frame around it, you start to see it differently. When your internal view changes, everything around you starts to change.

I remember telling my wife a while ago that I received a rhema word. A rhema word is a word from The Word - or a "now word" from God. She replied, "It's always been there." And she was right. It had always been there, but I had never seen it – until that moment...

I have learned to pay attention when this happens. I have found that when a verse catches my attention in this way, it is because God wants to give me a deeper revelation (divine insight and understanding) into the Scripture I am reading.

In this day and age, knowledge will not be enough to get you where God wants you to go. We need revelation. You may have a lot of information, but what you need is revealed knowledge. Revelation will cause you to walk in the perfect will of God. We have to be seers, not lookers.

One word from God can change everything. In II Kings 6, Samaria was experiencing a famine that was so severe that they were eating dove dung. Dove dung doesn't even taste good with cool whip! Dove dung was so valuable during those days that it sold for 5 shekels of silver.

When it became so bad that the people were turning to cannibalism, Elisha received a word from God. With confidence, he said, "Tomorrow about this time a measure of fine flour will sell for a shekel and two measures of barley for a shekel in the gate of Samaria! (2 Kings 7:1, AMP)

It seemed impossible. It seemed to be too good to be true, but sure enough, at the exact time Elisha predicted, the entire economy of Samaria shifted from extreme desperation to prosperity. One word from God is that powerful.

Because I've come to understand how the Word of God works, I have learned to pay attention to these moments. When I saw that phrase, "I looked," He spoke to me that there is more to it than we are giving Him credit for. He whispered to my heart to "tell my people they cannot afford to be looking any longer." I am going to begin to release a seeing generation. I am going to turn their looking into seeing.'"

You might say, "I'm going through hell!" I say, "Don't stop!" Just because you find yourself in a problem doesn't mean you should just give up and quit. Sometimes, people quit too quickly. Just one word from God can change everything. Try going through Matthew, Mark, Luke, and John instead. It will change your whole perspective.

There is more happening than what is obvious to the natural eye. We also see that in the story in II Kings 16:17. The Syrian army surrounded the city by night-the city that the prophet Elisha was living in. His servant got up early in the morning and looked outside the city walls only to see an army of horses and chariots about to scale the fortress. The servant was instantly consumed with fear.

What would you do if you were living in South Korea and woke up to see the North Koreans amassed at the border with missiles and tanks and an army in goose-step formation, brandishing their AK-47s and nuclear armaments? In the natural, you would have every right to panic. But Elisha refused to submit to his five senses. He was not going to cave into fear.

But, Elisha's servant continued to look at the problem. He was at his wit's end, convinced this bloodthirsty band of marauders would overcome them. "Alas, my master! What shall we do?" was his pleading query. But Elisha would not succumb to what was an obvious reality. Elisha answered, "Fear not, for those with us are more than those with them."

Elisha knew he didn't have an army to defeat the Syrians in the natural. But he did know his God had whatever and whomever he needed to gain the victory. And, the same holds true for you.

Keith Speak: "Some things don't even taste good with cool whip!"

Understand this: Elisha was already seeing something. He was seeing what the Syrian army did not see. He was seeing what his own servant could not see. He saw a great army. He saw a greater force surrounding a lesser force. He saw the answer.

"Then Elisha prayed, Lord, I pray You open his eyes that he may see. And the Lord opened the young man's eyes, and he saw, and behold, the mountain was full of horses and chariots of fire round about Elisha." There was a multitude of the heavenly host standing by to defend Elisha and his servant. The servant just needed eyes to see.

The Apostle Paul prayed the same way, "By having the eyes of your heart flooded with light, so that you can know and understand the hope to which He has called you, and how rich is His glorious inheritance in the saints (His set-apart ones)." (Ephesians 1:18, AMP)

How would you like your eyes to be so full of light that you could see in advance what the Lord has prepared for your life? He knows the plans He has for you – and they're good.

What are you choosing today? You can choose to trust. You can choose to ask God for revelation. You can wait on God for His perspective. You can ask to see. You can choose to look to your Solution instead of focusing on your problem. You have the power to choose.

Presidents and Olympians have the same 24 hours you have. They might have a team of aides around them. But they didn't start out that way.

They used what they had at the moment and polished their skills unseen by others. The violinist? Is he playing on a fiddle or a Stradivarius? He may have started out with the mundane, but his persistence to push through to excellence brought him the masterpiece. There are problems you will confront daily, but looking continuously at the situation instead of the solution will steal your joy and your peace.

There is joy in His presence. That's how you know you are with Him. We cannot deny that there are problems that you will face but there is a whole different way of looking at them that changes the situation.

BECOMING A SEER

Choose to set your mind on what causes you to have peace, and let Him show you what the place of peace is for you. Remember, revelation comes by the Spirit of God. You can ask for deeper revelation in any area you are lacking. You can choose to see beyond the obvious. Everyone can see what is obvious but I want to encourage you to take some time now to ask for revelation beyond the obvious, and watch how God moves you from looking to seeing!

I encourage you to take a few moments and write here any revelation that you receive as a result of your seeking Him. God is speaking, are you listening?

_____

_____

_____

_____

_____

_____

_____

_____

Chapter 4

SEEING YOUR LIFE AS IT REALLY IS

"May the eyes of your heart be illuminated, so that you may know what is the hope of His calling, and the wealth of the glory of His inheritance with the saints, and the preeminent magnitude of His virtue toward us." (Ephesians 1:18-19 NIV) As a hippie, I was used to people looking at me, and not seeing me. I could have let that determine who I became – but I didn't. If you are going to see and hear new things you have to ask God to open your eyes. He is displaying new and hidden revelations all the time but the eyes of your heart have to be open. You have to be able to see how God sees because man looks on the outward appearance but God looks on the heart.

Every January, I ask God to give me a new word. When is the last time you asked God to show you what He has for your future? Now's the time. I believe that God wants to move you into the unseen realm. It's so easy to look on the surface and not go deeper – but we don't live in a two dimensional world. We live in three dimensions – spirit, soul, and body. You can't see God in the natural, but He is there in the spirit. You can also connect with God through His word. His word is sprit and life. God's word is multi-faceted like a diamond. Because I know this, I have twenty-two different versions of the Bible on my iPhone. I believe that wisdom is the principal thing. With all that wisdom, I gain understanding. I want to see His word in all facets and in every way it is beingexpressed.

"When their eyes were instantly opened" (Luke 24, AMP). You can have information, just like you can have knowledge. But to hear what God is saying to you knowledge isn't enough – you must have the wisdom to know how to use that knowledge. You have to be able to discern the wheat from the chaff and what God is really saying to you.

I love the story of David and Goliath because David recognized a giant in his life when he saw it. David was able to see beyond the current state of affairs. He was able to see the potential in his life. He was able to see his life as it really was.

David saw the giant coming, but he did not run. Goliath was three times bigger than that young shepherd boy, and Goliath was a skilled, experienced warrior. David's only experiences had been with lions and bears, not a raging mass of flesh towering over him. That's like looking at someone fifteen feet high when you are just five feet tall, and expecting to have the advantage over him.

What piece of armament did David have to take down this monster? He had a mere slingshot, and some leather from an animal wrapped around a stick with a fork on it.

David spoke directly to his problem. He talked to the giant, telling Goliath he was facing the armies of the living God. It may have looked like all the odds were in this behemoth's favor, but that was just in the eyes of the beholder. The young Hebrew shepherd boy used the eyes of his heart to see beyond the fierce warrior that stood there, threatening his life and the lives of all his countrymen.

David unleashed his confidence with his mouth as an assault weapon, before he ever engaged the Philistine in a physical battle. In other words, David tackled his problem head on. David's attitude was defiant.

You see, every person in the midst of this situation had the opportunity to look at everything happening and draw his own conclusions. The Israelites looked and were terrified. King Saul looked at the situation and took the opportunity to coax someone into battling for him. David's brothers looked and saw David acting as a rogue. They accused him of being arrogant and wanting attention. Goliath looked and saw a ruddy youth three times smaller than he was. He also saw an easy target and a sure victory.

All of these people looked. But none of them could see. They did not see God getting ready to destroy the enemy. They didn't see God breathing on that stone as David released it. They couldn't imagine Goliath collapsing.

They did not see the boldness God was about to unleash on the children of Israel to pursue the Philistines for miles and completely destroy them. They could not see David's ultimate destiny and how this key victory was his launching point.

The Israelites could not see it, David's family could not see it, and King Saul could not see it. But David – a man after God's own heart could because he was a seer.

Though David saw the threat on his life standing right in front of him, he knew that God was on his side. He was aware that Goliath was neither threatening him, nor the Israelites. David understood that Goliath was really coming after God Himself. David was confident that God was with him– and he ran to the battle.

Just as David recognized the giant in life, God is calling you to do the same. One day, I took off my glasses and everything was fuzzy. I couldn't see a thing. But when I put them back on everything became clear. The same is true for you - you need to see. You need to see people the way Jesus sees you. Are you wearing your spiritual glasses? When you wear them, you will learn to see your situation for what it really is. You will find yourself walking in a boldness you never imagined.

What would you say the future would be like for a child given up for adoption who later dropped out of college to save money for his parents? While in college, he was homeless and slept on floors at friend's apartments. He turned in empty soda bottles for 5 cents so he could have money to eat.

He later said, "Success is all about grinding it out. I'm convinced that half of what separates successful entrepreneurs from the non-successful ones is pure perseverance." That young man became one of the most successful seers in the world - Steve Jobs. He was a creative genius. In fact, the Bible I read from every day came from his imagination, in an iPad, and this book was typed on a product that he dreamed-up too, a Mac. But if people were to judge Steve Jobs based on his outward appearance (jeans and black turtlenecks) they would not have seen the genius that he was. While he may not have looked successful at first glance – his story is one that highlights the importance of looking beyond the natural and seeing what you are meant to be.

BECOMING A SEER

1. **How do the people around you see you?**

2. **Are they right or are they just looking at the surface?**

3. **Do you feel limited by their vision of who you are?**

4. **How can you change the power others have over how you see yourself?**

Chapter 5

TURN ON THE LIGHT

Then Caleb quieted the people before Moses, and said, 'Let us go up at once and take possession, for we are well able to overcome it.'" (Numbers 13:30 NASB) I've seen people who have let the condition of life beat them down until they are ready to give-up. But that boy I saw on the street in Paris wasn't one of them. He still held to hope even though it didn't make sense. You look at your children and you wonder what will become of them. You look at your checkbook and you wonder where your next meal will come from. You look at your weight and you feel like a failure. But what if you were to take a step back and see at these things like God sees them?

In any situation you face in life, you always have two options: two reports you can believe. You can believe what your mind 'reports to you.' You can believe what you are able to reason and naturally see. You can believe others' 'take' on your situation or you can believe what God says. If you only look on the surface of situations in your life, you are limiting yourself and the vision God has for your destiny. Remember – God is able to see far beyond what you can ever imagine and His plans for you are good.

In Numbers, Joshua and Caleb set themselves apart because they refused to be subject to the reports of the Promised Land being "full of giants". When the other men trembled because they couldn't see a way out, Joshua and Caleb a different outlook on the land they would soon conquer. They refused to be imprisoned by anxiety, or stopped in their tracks by negativity. You may have been stymied by speeding ticket, high cholesterol, a divorce or a child on drugs but these issues don't have the power to barricade your mind and keep you from moving forward.

The ten spies looked at the worst parts of the situation and because they were focused on that, they didn't realize that victory was possible. Your glass is either half empty or half full, and theirs was completely devoid of anything. They came back from a land God had promised to give them, already defeated in their own minds.

These Hebrew children would wear their vintage clothing for forty years following their fearless leader Moses and yet, they were afraid to walk into their inheritance? What was wrong with their thinking? Had too much time in Egypt blinded their eyes to what the Lord had prepared for them?

Remember the spirit of fear that tried to paralyze the ten spies from receiving their inheritance? The negative reports they gave about the situation discouraged everyone else in the camp. Know this with certainty: the people you hang around are the people you are going to be like. You can see from this story, the power of negative influence. I encourage you to   choose your friends carefully. You are either an influencer or you are being influenced. There is no neutral ground.

There is a whole new dimension out there for you, once you cross over from looking to seeing. That is what the ten spies had to do but they needed heroes to stand up and challenge them, which is exactly what Joshua and Caleb did. Joshua inherited Moses' mantle and the Bible says Caleb had a "different spirit."

What was the different spirit that Caleb had? What made Joshua and Caleb say 'We are well able,' when everyone else was ready to surrender to the report of giants in the land? What did Joshua and Caleb see, that the other spies only looked at but could not perceive?

Everything you see in life has to do with your perspective. Think about it. If you are standing on a corner and witness an accident, from your one vantage point, you will see things from that one perspective.

But what if you are in a helicopter above the accident? Suddenly, you have more information. Now, you are able to see the entire event from start-to-finish. You can make an accurate judgment call. Now you have all the information you need.

When you have a spiritual perspective, you can see the situation clearly, because you are looking at it from your heart instead of your head. When you see from only one vantage point, your vision is limited. You will make a limited call from that limited perspective.

Caleb and Joshua had the expanded perspective because they believed in God's great power to accomplish what He was promising. The giants looked big to the other ten spies, because the spies compared the giants to themselves.

To Joshua and Caleb, the giants looked small. They were not comparing the giants to themselves. They were comparing the giants to the Almighty. In light of His power, the giants were mere grasshoppers. They were all looking at the same situation, but Joshua and Caleb had the higher vantage point. They weren't just looking... they were seeing.

These two warriors had the courage to stand up against ten very negative and tired compatriots, who were probably complaining that they even had to consider listening to another side of the story. But their whining and murmuring fell on deaf ears. Joshua and Caleb had a different vision in their hearts, combined with grapes as big as grapefruit on their shoulders.

The sight of such bounty was enough to make any tired Hebrew tribesman reconsider conquering more tribes. It is interesting that the fruit grown in Israel today is still huge, luscious and exported all over Europe and the Middle East? Both Joshua and Caleb had a heart to set their people free into a land long ago deeded to them by the Father Himself.

You might feel imprisoned by your past, or imprisoned by people who have told you there is no way out for you. They tell you that you have missed the mark for what you consider to be too long a period of time.

But, God has a plan of redemption and restoration tailor-made for you. You just need to realize that there is another way of looking at your life. It's a way of freedom and blessing, and a way where you are truly worshipping Him. It will bring you into a whole new reality of His presence.

There is always a way out. There is an answer to the quagmire you might be wallowing around in at the moment. But you have to make an effort to see that solution. Other people are not always going to do it for you. You have to stand up and "take the bull by the horns," and shake up the situation.

The greater One living inside you will show you what to do, and show you how to handle a tough situation, if you will only listen. The devil tries to persuade you to sit back and relax, whispering to your heart, and trying to make you believe your situation is hopeless. But rising up in your authority is your way out, seeing that you have God on your side, not just the enemy stealing from you.

Do not be deceived by the discouragement of the enemy and follow him back into darkness. Satan appears as an angel of light. He seems so good on the surface but he is actually the epitome of evil. He is the counterfeit of everything good and anything of God in the Universe.

Did you know that the Chinese character for the devil is a man hidden under a chair? That's how the devil works - his whole purpose is to lure you into fear and unbelief.

One of my favorite seers is Thomas Edison. He had over 1,000 patents issued in his name though he is most known for making the first commercially available light bulb. Now days, it seems like not such a big deal but have you ever tried to read a book by candlelight - it's not easy. Edison wasn't successful on his first, second, third or even nine hundredth try. He persevered and after more than 1,000 prototypes he created an invention that stood the test of time. Edison wasn't a quitter and he didn't listen to others who said his ideas weren't possible.

Edison said, "Many of life's failures are people who did not realize how close they were to success when they gave up."

That's not who you are – you're not destined to live life in the dark. It's time to "turn on the light" and see what God has destined for your life.

BECOMING A SEER

1. Was there a time when you allowed yourself to limit what you were doing because you didn't "turn on the light"? If so, how did you get out of that situation?

2. Are you in a situation right now that you aren't "seeing" right?

3. What can you do today to begin to see yourself and your situation the way God sees them?

Chapter 6

BE READY FOR YOUR DAY OF DESTINY

A lso He brought me by way of the north gate to the front of the temple; so I looked, and behold, the glory of the Lord filled the house of the Lord; and I fell on my face. And the Lord said to me, "Son of man, mark well, see with your eyes and hear with your ears..." (Ezekiel 44:4-5 NKJV) You have an appointment with destiny. God has an amazing plan for your life, and He has it timed perfectly. We don't always understand His timing, but as we trust in Him, we can look back across the events of our lives and see His absolute perfection in leading us.

Listen, your day of destiny will arrive and you need to make sure you are ready for it when it shows up. It is easy to grow weary as you wait on God for His promises to you. You have to trust that His timing is perfect. But, while you are waiting on Him, don't fall asleep.

In the early 1970's after I got saved I worked as a janitor at a small church in North Las Vegas. Pastor Bertie McCoy, from Oklahoma, was a dedicated woman of God. While I cleaned, I prayed – and Bertie encouraged me to never give up on the power of prayer. I was really concerned about my sister Janice. Janice was a top showgirl in Las Vegas and worked in the chorus lines. She was beautiful, smart, athletic, and broken. Addicted to drugs, Jan went out every night with celebrities. Combined with the methamphetamine use and lack of sleep, the lifestyle turned her into a shadow of her former self. She was let go from her hotel when she was down to 88 pounds. At 5' 9", with her ribs showing, she looked anorexic and had lost her spark. Jan ultimately ended up in a mental home and was left to die – but I was not willing to give up on her.

One day as I cleaned the church, she practically crawled into the church on her hands and knees. A shadow of her former self, she asked, "Do you think God can help me?" Weak and barely able to stand, I ushered her inside and said a resounding, "Yes!" I prepared a room for her and she stayed inside the church. Every service, she sat on the front row. One day, I was able to pray with her and get her set free of demonic activity. She married and had a beautiful daughter, Jennifer. Five years later, Jan became the associate pastor of that very church! She could preach like a house on fire and made the Old Testament come alive like People Magazine.

Jan crawled into that church on her hands and knees at the right time. God was there and her life was changed.

Keith Speak: "If you're late in the natural, you will be late in the spirit. Your natural life ia direct reflection of your spiritual Life"

God will give you direction. It may be through His still small voice. It may be mentors that He places in your life. Sometimes, these coaches/teachers/trainers may even seem to be hard on you. But understand if you have a word from the Lord for your life, there will be a season of preparation.

Esther was a young girl who became queen, and upon whose shoulders, the salvation of her nation would suddenly rest. She was born for that moment – but it didn't come easy and it took time. She had to wait and prepare. She was a young woman, exiled in a foreign land. She was also an orphan, raised by a loving uncle named Mordecai.

When she was just a teen, the King dismissed his queen for disobedience and began a kingdom-wide search for a new queen. It was mandated that every young, beautiful virgin woman be brought to him as a potential bride.

Esther was taken from her home and placed under the care of the King's eunuch, Hegai. Esther was favored and received special beauty regimens, a favorable place in the harem and more responsibility.

Long before her defining moment, Esther spent many hours learning the customs and ways of the palace. She had facials, hair care, massage, her nails were spot-on, her eyebrows perfectly arched. She wore the best clothes (not some knock-off imitations). Esther did not complain while she was being prepared – she enjoyed the process and the benefits while not allowing it to change who she was on the inside. She was a strong woman. She was the kind of girl who turned heads.

Eventually, she was chosen as queen and started her royal duties. Then, without warning, her moment arrived. A man named Haaman, in a high position with the king. He convinced the king to exterminate the Jews living throughout all of the provinces. The king agreed to do this without knowing his bride, Esther, was Jewish. Mordecai sent word to Esther and instructed her to go to the king to plead for her people.

Even though she was ready physically, Esther took the time to prepare spiritually. She spent three days fasting, preparing to ask the king her petition. It wasn't an easy assignment – in her day she could be executed for coming before the king without an invitation. It was an important day. It was a vital moment. When the King saw her coming through the door without his express permission, it would be the defining moment when he would determine if she lived or died, and ultimately decide the life of every Jewish person living in Persia at the time.

Her whole race could have been exterminated if the King decided not to favor on Esther her day of destiny. A nation of people hung in the balance. Her obedience, combined with the knowledge of God's favor on her life, proved to be a winning asset when the King chose her from thousands of women presented to him to stand by his side.

Boldly Esther declared, "If I perish, I perish." But she realized she was not just taking this petition in for herself. Esther had courage but she also prepared for success. She saw the threat, which stood in front of her but she also saw and understood that the glory should go to the Lord, who would anoint her efforts if she were obedient to His Word.

Esther did not just wait around in complacency for her moment. She submitted to the process of preparation.

Just like this Persian queen, you need to be prepared for your day of destiny. Preparation is natural and supernatural. If you don't take care of things in the natural, you won't take care of things in the Spirit. If you're always late, or unprepared in the natural, you will be late and unprepared in the Spirit too. Your practical life is always a reflection of your spiritual life.

One person who did not neglect her time of preparation was Laura Ingalls Wilder. Laura was raised on the prairie and grew up in a very small town. Her experiences growing up later became the material for a television series named for her books: *Little House on the Prairie*. This great American author didn't publish her first book until she was sixty-five.

It is clear to anyone who has read her books that her experiences on that little prairie formed her into a strong woman who was willing to do whatever was necessary to survive. But did you know that the first book she wrote entitled, *Pioneer Girl* was never published? Laura could have given up when her first work was rejected – but she didn't. And today millions have experienced what life was like when she was a child thanks to her story telling.

You may not always know when there's going to be a moment of destiny, or a trial. But if you have eyes to see, you will be prepared.

BECOMING A SEER

Often times it is helpful to look back and see where God has been there for you. It's amazing when you see where He has brought you from as a reminder of where you're going.

1. Is there a "word" God has given you about your destiny?

2. God's been preparing you for that destiny! Are you accepting of the time of preparation?

3. Thinking of the examples in this chapter (Esther, my sister Jan, and Laura Ingalls Wilder) how can you see that being prepared for the right moment is good?

Chapter 7

CLARITY

I pray for you constantly, asking God, the glorious Father of our Lord Jesus Christ, to give you wisdom to see CLEARLY and really understand who Christ is and all that He has done for you." (Ephesians 1: 16-17 TLB) There was a period of my life when I was "away" from the Lord, after I was first saved. I went to a church and they told me God put sickness on people to teach them something.

I was newly saved. But even though I did not understand the Word of God very much at the time, I knew enough about God to know that He does NOT do bad things. I knew He was a Father, who would not put sickness on His children.

It drove me out of the church and back into the fog. I lived in a gray area of being backslidden for about eighteen months because of that one comment. What I discovered was that when you're away from God, things are no longer clear-cut.

Keith Speak: "Look with your heart and not with your eyes... humanity is waiting."

When you have His word hidden in your heart, speaking, declaring and decreeing faith out of your mouth, your perspective is free, focused and panoramic. In this state of being, you can believe God for anything.

But when that dust starts to come in and settle on your dreams, things begin to look more vague and remote. Dust that vision off with your faith and stir yourself up - do not walk away.

When you have tasted of the good things of God and then depart, the enemy comes at you with a vengeance. You become confused, and the lines of your life are no longer black and white, but gray.

This confusion happens when you put down the Bible and allow other voices to start speaking to you. Many times this happens through offenses. Someone at church or another Christian may have offended you, so you start to withdraw and the enemy starts to move into your mind.

Like the serpent said to Eve in the book of Genesis. 'Hath God really said?" Well, yes He has, and His Word never changes.

But there are people today who have nothing to do with the Word, which is still the best-selling and most read book ever written. The Bible contains more than 5,000 years of wisdom that still works today!

So many people have missed a layer of life that they have tried to satisfy with every other kind of physical and emotional delight. But the pleasures of this life pale in comparison to the life of the Spirit that can be lived while you are right here on earth. You don't have to wait until you make that trip to heaven.

Jesus said, "The Kingdom of Heaven is at hand." In other words, God's perfect will has come close to you – even here on earth. You can experience God's perfect will if you can grasp (perceive, believe and lay hold of) what God is saying!

When I walked away from the Lord, my life went into a tailspin for nearly two years. The crazy part of it was, I thought I was having fun partying and traveling with my friends, doing risky things I would have never done when I was living for the Lord.

Of course in my mind, I thought this was a great time. Yet, even while I was acting crazy, I could never escape the sense of loneliness and the feeling that maybe I wasn't quite on the right track. I could never shake the sense that something in my life just didn't line up, although, at the time, I couldn't put my finger on it.

Finally, some friends invited me to church on my birthday, luring me back with my favorite lemon meringue pie, and it worked! Once I started to hear the Word preached again, and the Spirit of God started to speak to my heart, all the drugs, alcohol and parties in the world couldn't substitute for the peace Jesus restored to my heart.

People do ridiculous things because they have stepped away from the light. When you are in darkness, even a little light hurts your eyes. You have to keep cleaning your lenses if you want to keep seeing out of them.

Once God's word becomes alive to you again, your perspective becomes focused and even panoramic to the point that you start seeing things you never realized existed. Suddenly, you realize that there is a whole new world out there waiting to open up to you,

This is when you can start believing God for anything. Don't let the dust settle on your dreams and make them blurry, vague and remote. Stir yourself up and blast off the blurriness while your mouth speaks faith and your heart comes to the forefront with courage.

I don't know where you are right now and I don't know what you are doing. But I do know this, that God is bigger than your situation. He is big enough to forgive you and He has plans for your life. No matter the offense – no matter who's offended you or who you've offended – it's not too late for you to make it right. Forgiveness is a choice. You can choose to let it go, you can also choose to ask for forgiveness.

One of the great leaders of our time, former South African prisoner and president, Nelson Mandela said this, "Forgiveness liberates the soul. It removes fear. That is why it is such a powerful weapon."

You were set free from darkness once you walked into his marvelous light. The moment you asked Jesus into your heart, the darkness fled from your spirit. That's exactly what happened to me once I came back to God.

It just takes a mind renewal, a different point of view that the Word of God brings you. This Word has been a bestseller for two thousand years, and it keeps you flowing and moving in the Spirit and not bogged down with the woes of the world.

That is what wisdom and revelation is all about. You do not need more knowledge! What you do need is revelation about the knowledge you already have. That is exactly what happens when you see something or someone for what they really are: it is revealed knowledge from the Revelator Himself.

You don't need lens cleaners for your glasses when you have His wisdom. The clarity He gives you will cut through the blurry areas of your life and make your vision crisp. God will illuminate your path by His word and give you everything you need, for every decision, at every turn.

BECOMING A SEER

1. **Who do you need to forgive and why?**

2. **If you forgive, it will bring clarity to your life. Think about how God would view your offense. Ask Him to show you the "bigger picture". The answer may not come right away – but it will come.**

WALKING BY FAITH

S o we are always of good courage. We know that while we are at home in the body we are away from the Lord, for we walk by faith, not by sight." (II Corinthians 5:6-7 NKJV) Is your hope, faith and expectation set on the unseen? Have you learned to walk by faith and not by sight? Do you live life according to the realm of the Spirit, not according to appearances or what the natural eye can see? That's what being a seer is all about – learning to see with the eyes of your heart and not relying only on your natural vision.

There are pilots who fly Apache attack helicopters with amazing weapons systems. These guys put on a special kind of helmet to fly that helicopter. With one eye they fire their weapons. They see through a scope and they are able to see their target clearly. With the other eye, they see the natural world.

This is a wonderful way to explain how we live life here on earth and life live in the Spirit. As believers, we see into the unseen and fire our weapons out of that eye. With the other eye, we see our natural world. The two eyes work together to give us a real-time perspective on what surrounds us.

How long does it take to see two different things at the same time? How long does it take to navigate between the seen and the unseen? The brain has the capability to see and process between two differing pictures. And we are capable of seeing the seen and the unseen at the same time.

It takes training for these pilots to get used to it. They spend a lot of time practicing to be able fly and fight, simultaneously. It is in this same way that we live life by faith. With one set of eyes, our natural eyes, we see the seen realm, and with the other set of eyes, we see the unseen. We live in one realm and we war in the other one. You can fire spiritual weapons in the invisible kingdom of prayer: the unseen is greater than the seen.

Sometimes, we need to go into training. If you ever get a funny look on your face, you may be looking at the unseen.

How do we train? Here are a few steps to make you more aware of the unseen realm. Stay in the Word. The Bible is the culmination of all that God is saying. That way, you get a clear look into God's perspective on all of the different areas of life. You have access to the very wisdom and knowledge of God. Reading the Word also propels revelation.

According to the Romans 10:17, faith comes by hearing - hearing by the Word of God. That word 'hearing' has to do with revelation, perception and understanding. In other words, your ability to receive revelation and build your faith comes from the Word of God. The more you read God's word, the more your understanding and revelation will grow, and the more your revelation grows, the more your faith increases.

Another way we train is to pray. Prayer is expressed in many ways. You may pray in your regular language. You may pray in tongues. Prayer involves listening for God's voice. Prayer is also asking God for your needs and desires.

Regardless of how you pray, you need to pray. This communion and conversation with God strengthens your bond with Him and helps you remain in peace, no matter what situations you may face. Prayer and faith together are powerful combinations that move the hand of God.

Prayer and faith together are powerful combinations that move the hand of God.

In addition, you can train in praise and worship. When you combine the natural power of music with Spirit-inspired lyrics, and then you yourself begin to sing out with your voice, watch out! God inhabits the praises of His people, and the devil cannot stand to be in an atmosphere of praise. You literally drive out demonic forces when you open up your mouth and release praise.

When you begin to catch the perspective that God and His angels are working on your behalf, the devil is running in fear, you are seeing into the unseen. Your greatest weapons have been fired.

Keith Speak: "You say, 'Brother Hudson, I would never act the way you act.' That's your problem... you need to get delivered ... from yourself"

How do you connect between the two realms? How do you see the plans and purposes of God in the imperfect natural realm? You connect yourself from the seen to the unseen by words.

One lady in Mexico did this as missionaries stood around her and prayed for her baby to be healed. Even though they prayed fervently, nothing happened. But this mother would not give up. She rose up, started looking to heaven, and believed that God would bring life back to this infant when nothing else would work. Suddenly, that baby who had not breathed for several minutes, started to cry again.

When you are a Christian and you believe in an unseen God, you have an anchor for your soul. We have an anchor that reaches right into the Presence of God, and goes into the Holy of holies.

God is the God of the Impossible. When your fear screams, 'This is the end!' God says, 'Now I can take over where you left off!' Walking by faith is not a one-time event. Walking by faith means we consistently move in the realm of the supernatural. We draw from the unseen as a part of our 'normal' expression of faith and trust. And walking implies moving forward.

There may be times in life where you stand. Maybe, after having done all, that is all we can do, is stand. But most of the time, you are walking by faith. You are making decisions from a position of faith. When we are moving forward in our faith! When we learn to walk, we learn to walk towards something or someone – not backwards. It's the same in the Spirit!

"So we are always of good courage. We know that while we are at home in the body we are away from the Lord, for we walk by faith, not by sight." (2 Corinthians 5:6-7, ESV)

The first time I went out with my wife-to-be, Mary, it wasn't exactly a date. She was an ABC radio reporter in Las Vegas, NV, and had been invited to a dinner at the Stardust hotel celebrating the crew of the movie *Star Trek*. Being an ardent Trekkie fan myself, this sounded like a lot of fun, especially since the ultimate point of the night out would be to witness to the various celebrities attending.

As we sat down to a five-course dinner, the brother of then-President Jimmy Carter entered the room. Ah, thought my future wife, this will be a great opportunity to interview a sitting president's brother, Billy Bob, as he was known, and quite a character at that. And, after we finished the interview, possibly an excellent opportunity to witness.

So, after dinner, we presented ourselves to Billy Carter to see if we could ask him a few questions. He readily agreed, and Mary began to pellet him with queries.

Once the interview was over, she said to Carter, "Now my friend here has something he would like to give you." At that moment, I reached my hand into my suit coat pocket to grab a tract. Immediately, two secret servicemen jumped in front of me like lunging mountain lions, guns drawn, and said, "Now just take your hand out of your coat very slowly."

Of course, I did exactly what they told me to do, shocked to see such an immediate and violent reaction to such a simple move as me putting my hand inside my coat. As I carefully slid my hand out of my inside pocket, I pulled out a Charles Capps mini book entitled, *Your Words Hold Creative Power.*

They stood back somewhat dismayed at what they saw. They were looking at my hand, expecting to see a weapon; but what they didn't expect to see was a booklet designed to change Carter's life for eternity, as the result of their shakedown.

Those agents are trained to react instantly to the worst possible threat to the person they are protecting. It is part of their line of duty for them to look on the surface and anticipate a weapon emerging from someone's coat pocket instead of a Christian tract.

They instantly made a decision based on what they were looking at. They could not 'see' into my coat. They had no additional information or revelation regarding what I was about to do. Thankfully, they were also trained not to fire until the threat was actually a proven one.

Often times in life, we react to what we are looking at in the natural. Sometimes, we even think we are in danger when really it is nothing of the sort. We may find ourselves reacting in fear because we feel threatened, when we are simply passing through the 'shadow' of the valley. And we lash out with guns a blazing! And unfortunately, if we are looking with naturally eyes, we probably react from our flesh by yelling and screaming.

When we have the bigger picture – the God perspective – we can see both the natural picture and the supernatural picture. Instead of reacting to what we think is happening, we respond with a fuller understanding of what is actually happening.

If the guards had had the full picture, they would have simply watched as I handed him the booklet. In fact, if they had the full picture (the plan of salvation too!), they would have helped me hand it to him and applaud my gesture.

In the description of the spiritual armor at the end of Ephesians, the Bible says that faith is our shield, and that, as our shield, faith is able to extinguish every fiery dart the enemy aims at us

This is what I call the Faith factor. Faith is so powerful that when we use it as our shield in life, it stops a fiery arrow midflight, extinguishing it instantly as it falls to the ground, and causing it to utterly fail in its mission.

Sometimes life looks like it is falling apart. Maybe you received a bad report from your employer about the future of your job. You thought you were having a good day. But suddenly, your world is topsy-turvy.

That report pierces your confidence in God's goodness, and suddenly, there is a fire raging in your emotions. You begin to worry about the outcome before you have even had time to process what the news means. You are already racing in your mind about back-up plan B before you have even had time to pray about the situation.

It looks really bad in the natural. But what you don't see is that God already has a new job lined up for you in a better company – a promotion, a raise, and a company car.

Don't feel bad if you have judged a person or a situation in the past and your diagnosis has turned out to be completely wrong. Not saying that it didn't look totally right on the surface at the outset, but all of a sudden new facts come to light that flip the circumstance around like a pancake on a hot griddle.

An article in the 2012 New England Journal of Medicine demonstrates the natural effects of disaster when you are only looking on the surface and not probing any deeper. Naturally, other cancer experts have challenged the study, but the time-honored accuracy of this lofty group deserves respect. And for our purposes, it demonstrates the vast void created when a superficial study is not more closely inspected.

In fact what this investigation showed was that nearly one in three American breast cancer patients, actually 1.3 million women examined over the past thirty years, have been treated for tumors that would have never harmed them.

This comes out to as many as 70,000 women in the USA that may have been unnecessarily treated for this cancer, with a prognosis as severe as a double mastectomy, or removal of both breasts. The NEJM classifies this error as "over-diagnosis," but maybe they are demonstrating another classic case of looking on the surface of something without really seeing behind the veil?

However, not only is this a "classic" case but one that has unalterable results for thousands of women who have been drilled with a fear-filled description of what "could" happen to their bodies in the future. And just to be on the "safe" side, they were talked into maiming their bodies forever because a medical practitioner with natural authority has convinced them this is the only safe way to go. Time for a second opinion. Time to ask the Lord how He is looking at the situation.

Faith shields us in these moments. Faith, which is fueled by the Word of God, protects our hearts from the consuming fear that can ensue when life surprises. Instead of despair, and spiraling emotions, we are filled with hope.

Faith 'factors' the eternal perspective into our situation. The faith factor causes us to not jump to the conclusion based on what we are looking at. It causes us to praise, even when things look bad in the moment. It even reminds us of God's goodness and faithfulness in our past so that we factor that in to our evaluation of the situation!

BECOMING A SEER

1. **Has your faith been tested?**

2. **Are you walking by faith and working to see the hand of God in your situation?**

3. **How can you increase your faith by combining the seen with the unseen?**

Chapter 8

NOW IS THE TIME

For whatever is hidden is meant to be disclosed. And whatever is concealed is meant to be brought out into the open." (Mark 4:22 NKJV) Once, in the 1970's, I walked into an African-American gospel church. The intense preacher behind the pulpit was ON it. I could feel the flames of hell licking at the back of my legs with his non-stop singing and preaching. Every word that came out of his mouth invaded by spirit I was blown away by the power of his message – and what I was experiencing right then and there!

If you are always looking to what is going to happen in the future, you will never be responsible for the present. You say, 'I am waiting on God to do something in my future. But God says, I am waiting on you!"

When Moses faced the Lord at the edge of the Red Sea with six million Israelites following him, and Pharaoh's army waiting to destroy all of them, he cried out to God for help. But the Lord answered him, saying everything Moses needed to get across the Red Sea was already in his hand.

The Lord had given him a rod of authority with the walking stick he had placed in his hand. This long staff turned into a snake at a moment's notice, right in front of Pharaoh while Moses was still in Egypt. Even the magicians who saw it displayed in court right in front of them could not take this viper out. Moses' reptile was swallowing up their snakes.

In the face of this insurmountable supernatural power, Pharaoh finally let Moses and his people go. But, once the next obstacle of an impassable body of water presented itself to Moses and his six million followers, God said in effect, "Moses! Use your rod of authority (since its history definitely had demonstrated power over past situations) to part the Red Sea."

Listen; there is something in your hand right now that has demonstrated success to you in the past and God wants you to use it right now to push through your problems. Whether it is walking away from a victim attitude, rising up as a victor in front of what flaunts itself so violently in front of you, or just commanding the hurricane to back down in the name of Jesus, God had your solution taken care of the moment Jesus went to the cross. So get up, shake the dust off and ask Him, "Lord, what is it?" He will show you.

IT IS TIME TO SEE!

We need knowledge that is revealed to us from heaven for our lives, families and ministries.

Using what you have doesn't just mean something you can touch or hold, like Moses' rod. Using what you have can also mean releasing the revelation God has given you through your mouth.

You have something astoundingly powerful just south of your nose. James says the course of your entire life is set by your tongue, what you say. Your mouth is like a ship's rudder spiritually. Proverbs says that life and death are in the power of the tongue. That means you can speak life to the situation you see in front of you, and life will come. Or you can speak words of death, and death will ensue.

You may not have a talent or a special ability. You may not have a lot of money. You may not have a rod in your hand that turns into a snake. But, you do have a mouth…and you can speak. You can declare the Word of God. You can tap in to the promises of God. You release power and life into your situation, just by what you say. You don't have to wait for some great revival to see God move. You simply need to use what you have.

You don't have to wait for some mystical revival to see God move. You simply need to use what you have.

"Without prophetic vision people run wild, but blessed are those who follow God's teachings." (Proverbs 29:18)

Our generation has seen some of the greatest visionaries realize the incredible potential of their dreams. Among these incredible people are Walt Disney, Bill Gates, Steve Jobs, Mark Zuckerman, Henry Ford, Pablo Picasso, Thomas Edison and Dr. Martin Luther King, Jr.

Walt Disney got started living in a pastor's attic. He saw a mouse run across his bed one day. That mouse later became Walt's "Mickey Mouse". Most of us would have shot the mouse! But not Disney. Walt Disney was a seer!

Thank God for Bill Gates. Without him, we would not have the computers and the technological advancements we enjoy today. Steve Jobs didn't just sit and look at life. He did something about his vision! If it weren't for Henry Ford, we would still be riding bicycles.

Picasso's paintings are housed in museums all over the world. He saw something the world had never seen before and his style is both legendary and revolutionary. Picasso was a seer, not just a looker. One of his paintings recently sold for $165 million dollars.

George Washington and Mother Theresa – all visionaries – all seers – and I can go on!

So, Why Can't We Have Visionaries in the Church?

I believe God has saved some seers for this next generation. The time is now for these seers to arise!

Vision has nothing to do with your background, color or if you were raised on the street; The God inside of you is greater than all that. You can achieve anything if you believe.

You can view life by how your grandparents looked at it, or how Jon Stewart assesses it or how the Dali Lama sees it. But you will limit yourself because people are people. They aren't God and are not able see things the way He sees them. Lining yourself up with someone who lives and understands eternity can never be a bad thing. God sees your life, and His vision for it, from the beginning to the end.

God wants you to see the light. He desires that your eyes be opened. But you have to want it too. You have to be persistent and passionate in your desire to see people and situations the way He sees them, or the enemy will come back and keep biting you on your Achilles heel. He has studied mankind for thousands of years and learned our weaknesses. But he knows he is toast once we lean on God's strength and not our own.

Remember, Satan dwells in darkness; the way he sees God is perverted. Something may seem obvious to us as children of God, but it is not obvious to the enemy. And money is the last thing he wants you to have. But when you start ignoring his false humility to try to get you to think you are humble by exalting poverty. Instead, as you start listening to the Holy Spirit, you will start seeing His plan for your life. The One who created the universe will start to give you ideas, divine connections, witty inventions, books to be written and messages to be preached that will change your life and affect millions of people around you.

In Numbers 22, a donkey saw the angel, but Balaam was blind and kept ramming his trusty steed into the wall, obtrusive as the prophet was. Until the Lord opened his eyes (Num. 22:31) and he could see the Angel of the Lord standing in the way with his sword drawn.

Two chapters later, Balaam sees so clearly he is prophesying the future coming of Jesus Christ and telling everyone about it. "The man whose eye is opened speaks…." (Numbers 24:15)

Once the eyes of your heart are opened, life opens up to you in a whole new way.

It's like being in an area where you can't get cell reception. We've all been there. "Can you hear me?" "Can you hear me now?" Nothing is quite as frustrating.

God is greater than your past. God is greater than anything you've been through! And God wants to reach people through you.

I believe God is saying, "I'm waiting on you!" If you are always looking for something to happen in the future, then you will never be responsible for the present. We need to redeem the time we are living in. We need to understand and embrace this season and it starts with us seeing.

Some women in the church are looking for a mate in all the wrong places. They go after slick Willie. And you say, "Can't they see what will happen to them if they end up with that character?" What if you marry someone and you have only looked at him or her from the outside. Oh, they may be attractive but then, without really seeing them, you may wake up one day to find you have nothing in common. One of you wants to watch football game and the other one wants to go to the art museum.

Keith Speak: **"My wife and I have counseled many couples smitten with puppy love. This kind of romance can turn into a dog of a life."**

Seeing is not an option in this last hour. When you are seeing the signs of the Lord's returning it is going to produce urgency in you to preach the gospel to the ends of the earth, with a passion that drives you like fire on a dry landscape.

Our prayer for you is that you are able to see clearly, as it says in Ephesians 1:16-17, "I pray for you constantly, asking God, the glorious Father of our Lord Jesus Christ, to give you wisdom to see clearly and really understand who Christ is and all that He has done for you."

BECOMING A SEER

- Do others sway you? Do you settle for less than God's best for you?
- What can you do now to step into the calling God has for your life. Be concrete. Make a plan and stick to it.

Chapter 10

SEERS IN THE BIBLE

Formerly in Israel, when a man went to inquire of God, he aid, Come let us go to the seer for he that is now called a prophet was formerly called a seer." (I Samuel 9:9 NKJV) A prophet's revelation was primarily verbal while a seer's revelation is visionary. While the role of a prophet is familiar, we don't know as much about being a seer. A seer is a visionary prophet.

We need greater insight, discernment, and revelation. All real seers are prophets, but not all prophets are seers. A prophet can declare the Word of God, but not necessarily see what God will do. A seer does both and can also have dreams and visions. Both are prophetic but they have different capacities and dimensions.

Every person who is born-again sees with their physical eyes and the eyes of their hearts. God wants you to develop the second set of eyes... your seer eyes.

Let's look at some seers in the Bible.

ISRAEL (JACOB)

The patriarch of the Jews, Israel, had a key decision to make in his life. Was he going to move everything he had (his family, his goods) from a place that he had known all his life to live in a foreign land with a son he hadn't seen for years? Israel had no choice because of the famine but in Genesis 46:2-3, God confirmed His word with a vision.

"And God spoke to Israel in visions of the night, and said, Jacob! Jacob! And he said, Here am I. And He said, I am God, the God of your father; do not be afraid to go down to Egypt, for I will there make of you a great nation."

That vision gave Israel the courage to take on an unknown future.

PETER

"Peter went up on the housetop to pray, about the sixth hour. Then he became very hungry and wanted to eat; but while they made ready, he fell into a trance and saw heaven opened and an object like a great sheet bound at the four corners, descending to him and let down to the earth. In it were all kinds of four-footed animals of the earth, wild beasts, creeping things, and birds of the air. And a voice came to him, "Rise, Peter; kill and eat." But Peter said, "Not so, Lord! For I have never eaten anything common or unclean. "And a voice spoke to him again the second time, "What God has cleansed you must not call common." (Acts 10: 9-15)

Peter saw that God wanted him to make a change. Though he initially tried to resist that change, Peter realized that God wanted him to not rely upon the natural senses or the traditions of men – God wanted him to step into something new.

EZEKIEL

One of the great prophets of the Bible started out as not only a prophet – but also as a seer.

Now it came to pass in the thirtieth year, in the fourth month, on the fifth day of the month, as I was among the captives by the River Chebar, that the heavens were opened and I saw visions of God. (Ezekiel 1:1)

His prophecies still have tremendous impact on us today. His world about the valley of the dry bones is used as a wake-up call for a generation.

DANIEL

While he was only a youth, Daniel was a real seer. In fact, the word "visions" is mentioned eleven different times in his book of the bible.
When given the opportunity to eat the rich food of the king, he said no. He and his friends abstained from the food and became vegetarians.

Daniel 1:17 says, "As for these four young men, God gave them knowledge and skill in all literature and wisdom; and Daniel had understanding in all visions and dreams. Now at the end of the days, when the king had said that they should be brought in, the chief of the eunuchs brought them in before Nebuchadnezzar. Then the king interviewed them, and among them all none was found like Daniel, Hananiah, Mishael, and Azariah; therefore they served before the king. And in all matters of wisdom and understanding about which the king examined them, he found them ten times better than all the magicians and astrologers who were in all his realm."

WE ARE SEERS

In Acts 2:17, we are reminded that,

"…it shall come to pass in the last days, says God,
That I will pour out of My Spirit on all flesh;
Your sons and your daughters shall prophesy,
Your young men shall see visions…"

This scripture refers to us. If you are always looking for something to happen in the future, you won't be responsible for the present. God is waiting on you to do something with what you've been given. He's raising up seers in this generation. He's taking the "look" out of you and putting the "see" into you.

Being a seer has nothing to do with your background, color, or where you were raised. God inside of you is greater than that.

BECOMING A SEER

1. **What can you do today to begin to see the world around you as different?**

2. **Do you feel limited by your circumstance? If so, how can you change the way you see yourself?**

Conclusion

N *"Now learn this parable from the fig tree: when its branch has already become tender and puts forth leaves, you know that summer is near. So you also, when you see all these things, know that it is near-at the doors!"* (*Matthew 24: 32-34*) Everyone needs to have vision because vision is what sustains you.

Proverbs 29:18 reminds us, "Where there is no vision the people perish."

People run wild when they don't have guidance or vision in their lives. God's word provides a target for you to aim at. If you don't have a dartboard in front of you, you can never hit the bulls eye.

The Apostle Paul said that he did one thing… "I do not consider, brethren, that I have captured and made it my own [yet]; but one thing I do [it is my one aspiration]: forgetting what lies behind and straining forward to what lies ahead, I press on toward the goal to win the [supreme and heavenly] prize to which God in Christ Jesus is calling us upward. So let those [of us] who are spiritually mature and full-grown have this mind and hold these convictions; and if in any respect you have a different attitude of mind, God will make that clear to you also."

John wrote the whole book of Revelation as a seer.

Get into the spirit and release the true revelations of Jesus in your life. This generation is crying out for you to see them the way God sees them.

They don't care how much you know, they just want to know that you love them.

BOOKING

KEITH & MARY HUDSON MINISTRIES
P.O. Box 50937
Irvine, CA 92619
Tel: (951) 522-8391
Fax: (951) 894-5080
bookingthehudsons@gmail.com

keithhudson.org